Your Mother Wouldn't Like It

Your Mother Wouldn't Like It was compiled by Gillian Appleby with contributions from Peter Corey, Bob Hescott and Gail Renard.

The cast of the second television series of *Your Mother Wouldn't Like It* from the Central Junior Television Workshop are: Richard Allenson, Julian Aubrey, Karl Collins, Ashley Cowdrey, Richard De Sousa, Alison Dury, Pui Fan Lee, Stacey Green, Tessa Harrison, Oliver James Hawker, Ian Kirkby, Karen Murden, Christiana Norris, Julie Schatzberger, Dena Snelgrove, Tim Stanley, Paul Stark, Philip Wombwell, Phoebe Wood.

Your Mother Wouldn't Like It

Based on the Central television series

Illustrated by Paul Cemmick

DRAGON
GRAFTON BOOKS
A Division of the Collins Publishing Group

LONDON GLASGOW
TORONTO SYDNEY AUCKLAND

Dragon
Grafton Books
A Division of the Collins Publishing Group
8 Grafton Street, London W1X 3LA

Published by Dragon Books 1986

This publication is based on the television series *Your Mother Wouldn't Like It* produced by Central Independent Television Plc.

ISBN 0-583-31087-7

Printed and bound in Great Britain by
Collins, Glasgow

Set in Plantin

CONTENTS

LOAF'S DAYDREAMS...
LOAF IS BOND
SECRET AGENT 006½
LICENSED TO BE AN IDIOT!
FROM RUSSIA WITH LOAF
M.I.5. MOLE

1

JAMES BOND

'Read all about it!' shouted the newspaper man on the corner. 'Man arrested for spying in Iceland. Ice-spy scandal!'

'A spy,' thought Loaf as he walked past the newsstand. 'I could be a spy. I can just see me as James Bond – fast cars, fast women, fast action . . .'

The door to the outer office burst open and Bond entered, suave and sophisticated as ever.

'Morning, Miss Spendapenny,' he called to the secretary behind the desk.

'Good morning, James,' she breathed in reply. 'It's wonderful to see you again. How about a cosy dinner for two tonight so you can tell me all about your daring escape from man-eating goldfish on your last mission?'

'Now really, Miss Spendapenny,' Bond answered, checking his reflection in the mirror, 'you know I can't have dinner with you. It would ruin my image. Is M ready to see me yet?' he went on. 'I knew him when he was only L, you know.'

'He'll see you now,' said Miss Spendapenny with a sigh. Bond pushed open the heavy door and entered M's office.

M was sitting behind the desk with a paper bag with holes cut in it over his head.

'New look, eh?' said Bond cheerfully. 'You had a Harrod's bag last time. Is brown in fashion now?'

'Don't be stupid, Bond,' snapped M. 'The other one went all soggy when I got caught in the rain last week, so I had to get a new one. No one must ever know my true identity,' he continued in a lower voice, 'or the safety of the country could be at risk.'

'Risk?' repeated Bond. 'Good game, that. I took over the whole of Asia last time I played . . .'

'Bond!' roared M angrily. 'I'm talking about national security, not board games! I have a mission for you.'

'OK, M, hit me with it,' said Bond.

M reached across the desk and bashed Bond on the head with a rolled up sheet of paper. 'Whatever you want, Bond. But I've still got a mission for you. Read these instructions.'

Bond took the paper and read: 'Two pounds of sugar, one packet of chocolate biscuits, a jar of coffee . . .'

M snatched the paper back again. 'That's my shopping list,' he cried. 'Here, digest this.' He handed Bond another sheet of paper.

Bond folded the paper up and put it in his mouth. He chewed a couple of times and then gulped it down.

'What are you doing, Bond?' gasped M.

'Digesting it, sir,' Bond replied.

'Good grief,' groaned M, clutching his head and making the paper bag rustle. 'Listen, Bond,' he went on when he'd pulled himself together. 'We want you to track down the Smirsch gang, who are hunting the Slime organization, because they have invented the XTA620 Gamma Ray Gun and threatened to use it on the Muck Syndicate, who've threatened to use it on the Cringe Corporation – oh, and at the same time, can you save the world? Follow me, Bond?'

'I think so, sir. What you mean is, I've got to wreck a couple of buildings, smash up a few dozen cars, be charming to several pretty girls and crash some motor boats?' asked Bond.

'Spot on,' replied M. 'So you'll be needing all your usual tricks and devices to help you with your plans. I'll ask Q to come in and show us his latest gadgets.'

Two minutes later Q entered the room. He had a

Mickey Mouse mask over his face and he was carrying a large pile of gadgets.

'Now look here, Bond,' Q began. 'You know how expensive this equipment is, and I don't want you to treat it in your usual slap-dash manner. This wristwatch, for instance, has a built-in guided missile which will shoot straight up the nose of the person you fire it at. It's very effective, and I should know,' he said, raising the mask enough for Bond to see a nose blocked by two miniature missiles, one in each nostril.

'Next,' said Q, 'is a pen which works as a homing device, a nerve gas dispenser, a pistol, a fridge and a clock-radio. Treat it with care.'

Bond took the pen. 'Does it write?' he asked, scribbling on the nearest bit of paper. The sound of pop music filled the room.

'Don't be ridiculous,' snapped Q as he grabbed the pen and switched it off.

After quickly showing Bond the rest of the equipment, Q reached into his pocket and pulled out the final gadget.

'It looks like an orange,' said Bond when he saw the item.

'It's meant to,' replied Q. 'It may turn out to be the most useful gadget of all. It's a gas grenade. When you throw it at someone, it will release laughing gas which will have your enemies rolling on the floor, completely helpless with giggles. So long as you hold your breath you won't be affected, and you should be able to escape with ease.'

Bond took the orange and slipped it into his pocket.

'Now, Bond,' said M, searching through the papers on his desk till he found the one he wanted. 'Here are your instructions. You're to take a plane from Heathrow . . .'

'Do I have to take a plane?' asked Bond. 'Last time I

took a jumbo jet and there was the most awful row about it. They said I should have gone as a passenger, not stolen a plane, whatever my orders were.'

M groaned with despair. 'Go as a passenger, Bond,' he said. 'Here are your tickets. You will fly to Peepong, an island near Japan, where you will meet up with our agent OXO. He will help you to find the Gamma Ray Gun.'

'OK,' said Bond. 'When do I leave?'

'You'd better set off straightaway,' replied M. 'But be careful. The enemy could be after you from the minute you leave this building.'

Moments later Bond was outside on the pavement. He began walking towards the tube station, but soon he noticed that someone was following him.

'Just as well Q gave me the orange grenade,' thought Bond, reaching into his pocket for it. As he raised his hand to throw the grenade, a voice called out, 'Stop! Stop at once . . .'

'Stop! What do you think you're doing? Just look at this mess.' Loaf turned round quickly and discovered that he was standing in the middle of a heap of oranges. They had clearly fallen from the market stall beside him.

'What are you playing at?' yelled the angry market stall owner. 'Why did you take the one from the bottom? You're going to stand here and put the whole lot back up into a pyramid again, however long it takes you!'

Loaf looked sheepishly at the orange in his hand. 'I wish it really *was* a laughing gas grenade,' he said, as he began to pick up the oranges around his feet.

THIS IS THE LAND OF
THE JOLLY GREEN GIANT
FLUSH HIM OUT WITH
BIG-BLOW HANKIES
SNORK!
HO! HO! HO!
SEE THOSE BOGIES GO WITH BIG BLOW
BIG-BLOW
Store so much in so little

TWEEMAN

'MORE FUR THAN USUAL'

Once upon a time there was a lovely pink fluffy wabbit –

Help! I'm trapped inside a fairy story. Whoops, Toilet Door's coming back –

The bunny wabbit's name was treacle because he was so sweet –

It's all right, Toilet Door's gone again. This is me, Tweeman, Disaster of the Universe, magicked into this yucky yarn by the devilish Toilet Door. While he's not here I'll explain what happened. He phoned me up and bleated out some tale about being ill in bed with Weaselpox and would I go round and cheer him up with a story. Out of the goodness of my heart I did. What a con! I started reading Betty Potty's '*The Tale of Treacle Bun the Wabbit*' when I went all funny. The page began to spin before my eyes and the next thing I knew I was actually in the story as Treacle Bun's Mum! Oh no, here's Toilet Door again –

Treacle Bun the wabbit looked at the delicious mess of turnip tops and marshmallows the crafty fox was cooking and said –

What a load of bilge. Well, don't just sit there reading this story, get me out! Yes, you! You lot reading this rubbish. What? Well, I don't know how you can rescue me, I've never been stuck in a sickly saga like this before. What's that, Beverley Spiff of Churdle St. Neeves? Try some magic? By the powers of numbskull, of course I'll try some magic, but what magic do you suggest? Hang on Beverley, I can't hear you, Warwick Dingle of Bootle is trying to read and watch telly at the same time. One or the other please Warwick – oh charming. He's turned up the telly and closed the book. Sorry, you were saying, Beverley? Lift my magic sword above my head and say 'By the powers of grey scum?' Yes, that would certainly

break the Toilet Door's spell, but maybe it has escaped your notice, Beverley, that as Treacle Bun's Mum I am a weak and wobbly wabbit with paws. Not much steaming use when it comes to waving flaming swords around! All rights, I'm sorry, don't sulk. I think your suggestion has given me an idea. Hold it, Toilet Door's back – blow, he's sitting down now. Hang on, maybe I can send him to sleep with this endless epic –

So Treacle Bun the wabbit got away by the merest whisker and he hoppity hopped all the way home. Hoppity hop, hoppity hop, hoppity hop, hoppity hop, hoppity hop, hoppity hop, hoppity hop, hoppity hop, hoppity hop, hoppity –

He's asleep. I said he's – oi! You lot, don't go to sleep! Quiet now, I don't want him to wake up. Sssh! Who's that tap dancing in wellingtons? It's you, Keith Nasel of Louth – I don't care if you *have* got pins and needles, be quiet! Look, here's what I want you to do. Go to the kitchen and confront your Mum. Stand before her and cry, 'Great Lady of the Pinny, I crave a boon. Lend to me a spoon from the fabled canteen of cutlery.' Go on, I'll wait here – oh, and if you think about it, bring me back a carrot –

So Treacle Bun's Mum tucked him into his pyjamas and popped him into his bed of warm hay and potato peelings –

You're back, good. What? No, a pickled onion is not the same as a carrot, thank you Jonathan Bilge of Tintagel. Never mind, did you all get spoons? All right, Bruce Dimm of Eakring, a spatula will do. Now take your spoon or spatula and tuck it down the back of your neck – oh, I'm sorry if it's cold, Wendy Wart of Bishop Auckland, only d'you mind moving yourself? Now, everyone out into the garden, then at the top of your lungs shout, 'By the Powers of Grey Scum!' Pull out the spoon and wave it above your head. Do this three times, then begin the spell-breaking break dance, but get back inside before the neighbours send for an ambulance. Off you go, all of you. I'll stay here and twiddle my paws –

But before Treacle went to sleep old Mrs Treacle brought the bunny wabbit a mug of warm milk and a plate with four small bright orange baby carrots on it –

Mm, makes me quite peckish. Aaah! Don't creep up on me like that, you made me jump. Have you done it? Great! Yes . . . Yes . . . The magic's beginning to work . . . I'm coming out of the story. I'm ceasing to be a mangy Mummy wabbit, I am once more Tweeman, Disaster of the Universe! Oh, you've woken up have you, Toilet Door? That's right, cringe! I am free, thanks to these readers. Many thanks, and there's just one more thing I have to say – Tracey Dimple of Potter's Bar, do you always read in the bath? Too late to blush now, Tracey! Right kids all together – *Tweeman!*

LOAF'S LAUGHS

Loaf thinks a bolt from the blue means running away from a policeman!

Loaf's found a new way to make money. He wants to open a shoe shop so he's planted some shoe trees.

Loaf's only got one aim in life, but he missed!

Loaf was amazed when the ticket man on the bus collected the money and handed out the tickets in half a second. Loaf reckoned he must be a lightning conductor.

What's black and white and called Spot?
Loaf's pet zebra.

What would you get if you crossed Loaf with a monkey?
A stupid monkey.

Loaf tried glass-blowing, but he inhaled and got a pane in his stomach.

How do you confuse Loaf?
Put him in a circular room and tell him to stand in the corner.

Teacher: If you add 226 and 479, then double it and divide by 5 and add 17, what do you get?
Loaf: The wrong answer.

Last week Loaf changed his mind, but the new one didn't work either.

Loaf took up tap dancing but he broke his leg when he fell in the sink.

Loaf wanted to become a sea scout but his tent sank.

Doctor: You look hot and flushed, you must have flu.
Loaf: No, I walked.

Loaf's Mum: Loaf! Why has it taken you over an hour to fill that salt-cellar?
Loaf: Sorry, Mum, but the holes in the top are so small it's hard to get the salt in.

Producer: How do you manage to do so many stupid things in one day?
Loaf: I get up early.

Mr Briefcase knocked on Loaf's door early one morning and Loaf answered it, wearing his pyjamas and looking tired.

'Sorry, Loaf,' said Mr Briefcase. 'Did I wake you?'

'It's alright,' said Loaf sleepily. 'I had to get up to answer the door anyway.'

A jumbo jet crashed into Loaf's house last week. He'd left the landing light on.

Loaf pays half price on the bus because he isn't all there.

Loaf wants to be rustler but he can't find enough cellophane.

Producer: How do you suppose Princess Diana knew when she was going to have a baby?
Loaf: That's easy. It was in all the papers.

Loaf was visiting his cousin on a farm and admired one of the cows.

'It's a lovely colour,' said Loaf.

'Yes, it's a very expensive Jersey,' replied the cousin.

'Oh,' said Loaf, 'I thought that was its skin.

Loaf saw a sign on a lift which said, 'This lift will only take four people.' So he waited half an hour for another three to turn up.

Loaf was told to get two saxophones for tomorrow's show. He turned up with two bags of British Telecom rejects!

Loaf bought some rubber gloves so that he could wash his hands without getting his fingers wet.

One day Mr Briefcase found Loaf holding a rabbit by the neck. He was staring into its eyes and saying, 'What's five and five? Go on, what's five and five?'

'Loaf!' cried Mr Briefcase. 'What are you doing? Why are you shaking that rabbit by the neck?'

'Well,' said Loaf, 'I heard that rabbits multiply rapidly – but this one can't even add up.'

Loaf got marooned on a desert island. One day the tide washed a large rowing boat ashore. Loaf broke it up to build a raft.

Loaf thought his teacher like him. She kept putting 'x's in his book.

Loaf walked twenty miles to do his shopping. He was making his money go further.

Loaf: Is it right to say that you water a horse?
Loaf's Mum: That's right, dear.
Loaf: Then I'm going to milk the cat.

Loaf had two horses which he was very proud of, but he had one problem – he couldn't tell them apart. He tried all kinds of ways to distinguish them. He cut one's tail, but then the tail grew and he couldn't tell the difference again. Then he knocked a front tooth out of one of them, but the other had an accident and lost its front tooth as well, so Loaf couldn't tell them apart any more.

Loaf thought and thought, and finally he had an idea. He would measure the two horses. That solved the problem. He discovered that the black horse was an inch taller than the white one.

Loaf fell asleep one night with his head under the pillow. The fairies came and took out all his teeth.

SHARON, KAREN, DARREN... ...AND GARY

1

'TOP OF THE POPS'

Sharon, Karen and Darren all come from different directions, and meet up with Gary, who is plugged into a huge personal stereo which is almost bigger than he is! Gary taps his foot wildly out of time to some beat, not really noticing Sharon, Karen and Darren!

KAREN: Hello Sharon!

SHARON: Hello Karen!

KAREN: Hello Darren!

SHARON, KAREN AND DARREN: (*turn to Gary, together*) Hello Gary!!

From Gary there is: Nothing! The others turn back to Darren, and see that he is proudly holding a new twelve inch single record.

DARREN: I've got a new picture disc! (*Darren takes the disc out of its sleeve*) Have a look, Sharon?

Darren passes the disc to Sharon, and Sharon looks at the disc with interest, and then passes it on.

SHARON: Have a look, Karen?

Sharon passes disc to Karen. Karen's turn to study disc.

KAREN: Have a look, Darren?

Karen passes disc back to Darren, who now passes it to Gary.

DARREN: Have a look, Gary?

Darren passes the disc to Gary. Gary throws the disc away like a frisbee.

We hear the sound of a record breaking! Darren sighs.

SHARON: Sorry!

KAREN: Was that one of those new charity records, Darren?

DARREN: Where the money goes to some charity, Karen?

KAREN: No, where it's a charity to listen to it, Darren.

DARREN: I don't know. But it was a twelve inch record, Sharon.

SHARON: (*Looking towards the record's remains*) Not any more, Darren.

KAREN: Do you have a lot of records, Darren?

DARREN: (*wistfully looking towards the broken record again*) I used to, Karen.

KAREN: I've got hundreds of twelve inch, seven inch, and picture discs, Darren.

SHARON: So do I, Karen.

KAREN: Do you, Sharon?

SHARON: Yes. Mind you, it's all the same song. They just keep bringing it out in different sizes, Karen.

DARREN: We've got a new compact disc player at our house, Sharon.

SHARON: Straight up, Darren?

DARREN: And it's really tiny, Sharon!

KAREN: How does your compact disc player sound, Darren?

DARREN: I don't know. It's so compact we can't find it, Karen!

Sharon sighs.

SHARON: I think we'd better be going now, Darren.

DARREN: Why, Sharon?

SHARON: Because Gary's got to write another letter of advice to Bob Geldof, Darren. (*big sigh*) He's so dishy, Karen!

DARREN: Who? Bob Geldof, Sharon?

SHARON: No! GARY, Darren!

Sharon, Karen and Darren start to walk off. Gary still stands, glued to his spot, unseeing!

DARREN: Let's go and scratch some of Gary's records, Karen.

TAPEWORM'S TEASERS

Why did the chicken cross the road?

To prove he had guts.

LOAF'S DAYDREAMS...
GRRRR!
GRRR!
RUMBLE! RUMBLE!
SQUELCH!
GRRR!
INDIANA LOAF
AND
the GERBILS of DOOM

2

Berky Jones

Loaf was walking down the street when he noticed a large poster advertising the latest Indiana Jones movie. He stopped to read it.

'Come and see the most exciting film of the year,' he read. 'Enjoy the thrills, spills and action-packed adventure of *Indiana Jones and the Trip to Terror*.'

'I wish I could have some action-packed adventures,' thought Loaf. 'I'm sure I could be a big hero like Indiana Jones . . .'

The door to the little bar in downtown Istanbul swung open and in walked a tall, rugged, handsome man with some stamps stuck to his forehead. A woman at the nearest table stood up.

'Mr Jones, I presume,' she greeted him.

'My fame runs before me,' said Jones with a smile.

'And so does everything else, Berky,' said the woman. 'I can call you Berky, can I?'

'Be my guest,' Berky replied.

'No, it's alright. I've had my holidays,' the woman replied. 'Let me introduce myself. I'm Professor Peabody. I'm an archaeologist.'

'That's funny, so am I,' said Berky in surprise. 'How strange that we should meet up in a place like this.'

'It's not strange. I sent for you, remember?' the Professor told him.

'Oh, so you're the person who ordered me from the mail-order catalogue,' said Berky, fingering the stamps. 'I wish they'd find a better way to deliver us though. It's pretty tough trying to get into the postbox. What can I do for you?'

'First let me get you a drink,' said the Professor.

A waiter brought the drinks and Berky took a big gulp of his. 'Urgh!' he spluttered, spitting it out again. 'That's terrible!'

'Yeah, I thought it might be,' said the waiter.

'What is it?' asked Berky.

'A squeeze of lemon, a twist of pepper and a shot of gerbil piddle,' replied the waiter.

'Ah – no ice,' declared Berky, handing his glass back. 'That's what's wrong.'

'Come and sit down, Berky,' said the Professor impatiently, 'and I'll tell you why I sent for you.'

'I aim to as soon as I can find a chair without arms, so's I can turn it around and sit on it back to front,' Berky told her. He found a chair, but as soon as he sat on it the chair collapsed and Berky sprawled on the floor.

'No matter,' he cried, leaping to his feet. 'I'll just sit on the edge of this table.' As Berky placed his bottom on the table edge however, it tipped up and deposited him on the ground.

'Really Berky,' snapped the Professor, who was getting annoyed. 'Why can't you sit on a chair normally.'

'Oh, I couldn't do that,' said Berky, shocked. 'It would ruin my cool image.'

Finally Berky was seated and the Professor was able to begin.

'I expect you're wondering why I got you to come here today,' she said.

'No, I never even thought about it,' Berky answered with a grin.

'Good grief,' sighed the Professor. 'Berky, what do you know of a Hittite god called Mockers and his sandwiches of doom?'

'My gosh!' gasped Berky. 'Nothing – why?'

'Well, I found some ancient documents in a museum

here in Istanbul, and they say that the sacred Golden Toasty of Mockers is hidden in the middle of the Picknose jungle. It is solid gold and priceless, and I want you to find it for me.'

'Wow!' said Berky. 'But why do you want me to go? Why not go yourself?'

'Because there are hundreds of miles of jungle, swamps and rivers to cross to reach the spot, and it would ruin my hairstyle. Now, here is your map,' she said, holding out the chart for Berky to see. 'You had better set off as soon as you can – oh, and watch out for the Tea Tribe.'

'Who are they?' asked Berky nervously.

'They are the natives who live in the jungle,' the Professor told him. 'They worship Mockers and they get very offended if anyone tries to take the Golden Toasty. They toast intruders, then cut them in half and spread them with jam.'

Berky gulped.

'Now off you go,' said the Professor, pushing him towards the door. 'See you in a few weeks, with the Golden Toasty.'

In the days that followed Berky forced his way through the dense foliage of the Picknose jungle, struggled through the steaming swamps and sploshed through raging rivers. He fought alligators, snakes, and a few dozen tribes of Picknose pygmies. All in all his adventures were to excrutiatingly boring to relate. At last he emerged into a jungle clearing and spotted a totem pole standing in the centre. Fastened around it, on a gold chain, was the fabulous Golden Toasty of Mockers.

'Gosh!' gasped Berky, taking in the marvel before him. 'I must be the first human being to see this for centuries . . .'

A noise in the undergrowth make him look round.

Hundreds of natives were standing around him, spears in their hands and ferocious expressions on their faces.

'Oo-er,' moaned Berky. 'What am I going to do now? I don't want to be toasted by the Tea Tribe.'

Suddenly the natives parted to let a new arrival through. There was no mistaking the man with the chains of gold around his neck.

'Mr T!' Berky shouted in surprise. 'What are you doing here?'

'Hey, man!' cried Mr T. 'Welcome to the jungle. I think you met the Mr T Tribe already.'

'Mr T Tribe?' said Berky, amazed.

'Yeah, they been helping me find a new ornament for my person. Hey, there it is!' shouted Mr T and he pushed past Berky and went to remove the Golden Toasty from the totem pole. 'I been looking for this,' he said as he put it around his neck.

'That's not fair!' cried Berky. 'I've been through swamps, snakes, crocodiles and Picknose pygmies to get that treasure – besides, it should be booby trapped.'

Just then the totem pole creaked, swayed, and fell down to hit Berky on the head . . .

'Oof!' gasped Loaf as he sprawled on the pavement. He looked around quickly for Mr T, but all he saw was the lamppost he had just walked into. 'Oooh,' he groaned as he climbed to his feet again. 'Maybe I can do without action-packed adventures.'

CENSORED

TEMPERATURE?
HEADACHE?
RUNNY NOSE?
SORE THROAT?
ACHING LEGS?
IF SO...

STAY AWAY FROM ME. O.K.?
KEEP OUT!

PALACE HILL THE BOOK

PART 1

It was an ordinary Monday morning. Ordinary . . . but different. In fact, it wasn't ordinary at all. I don't know why I said it was. I'll start again. . . .

It was a Monday morning.

'It's Monday morning,' thought Prince William, as he drew back the curtains and looked out over Kensington. Immediately he felt guilty. He knew that his father would tell him off for drawing the curtains. There a special person whose job it was to draw curtains and, if William drew his own curtains, it would, according to his father, upset the Status Quo. This was something William could not understand. How could the fact that he'd drawn his own curtains upset a Rock Group? Did it have anything to do with his mother liking Duran Duran?

'I'll discuss it with my Social Studies teacher when I get back to school,' he thought. School! Of course. That was what was so special about this particular Monday. It was the first day of the autumn term at Palace Hill Comprehensive School, the school to which William and his younger brother Harry had been going for almost a year.

A year? Was it really that long? Probably not. It hardly seemed five minutes since the two Princes were first driven out through the large imposing gates of Kensington Palace, only to arrive some time later at the small, unimposing gates of Palace Hill. But what a five minutes it had been! Or what a year – whichever it was. William had always had trouble with 'time', mainly because there was a special person whose job it was to look after all that side of things. Oh, he had been given a watch for his birthday, but he hadn't worn it because it said on the box, 'Works perfectly under water,' and William couldn't swim. When he was King, he would employ someone to wear it for him.

He noticed his Palace Hill uniform, which the new nanny had laid out on a chair. She had only been with them since the hols. That was when Nanny Barnes had left to marry her nice policeman. Her name was Mary Goats (the new nanny, not the policeman!), and she seemed very pleasant. William sighed and slowly got dressed. He was just tying his tie (a Windsor knot, of course), when Harry came into his room.

'Wotcha, Dumbo!' said the younger Prince, quickly slipping into the Palace Hill way of talking. This was a side-effect of comprehensive education that their parents had not anticipated. They had spent many hours on the family holiday in Scotland, trying to persuade their sons to speak the Queen's English, but had failed, even though they had access to the genuine article!

But, apart from that, what a holiday it had been.

Getting up whenever they wanted, going to bed whenever they felt like it, watching any old rubbish on the television. That was the most difficult thing – there had been so much to choose from. William had seen things he didn't even realize existed. '*News at Ten*', '*Mastermind*' . . . and the great family favourite had been watching '*The Price is Right*' and trying to guess the price of things. Any member of the family who got within a thousand pounds of the right answer won a prize. Harry had been very crafty and got one of the servants to help him. Consequently he had done rather well, and won two racehorses, a Corgi, and some bits of Berkshire.

The breakfast gong brought an end to any further reminiscences, and, large plates of eggs, bacon, mushrooms, kippers, tomatoes, kidneys, sausages, toast and fried bread later, the two Princes were standing, more or less, on the forecourt of the Palace, waiting for the chauffeur to bring the car round. The chauffeur arrived on foot to explain that there was no car available. William was not amused.

'What about the black one?'

'Being serviced, Your Highness.'

'The big red one?'

'Being washed, Your Highness.'

'The even bigger blue one?'

'Ashtrays are full, Your Highness.'

'What about the funny-looking one with the foreign name?'

'I believe she's on a cruise, Your Highness.'

'I think he meant the funny-looking car,' interjected Harry.

'Oh. Your mother needs it for shopping, Your Highness.'

'Why don't we walk?' suggested Harry, who had tried walking in Scotland and rather enjoyed it.

'Walk?' William was appalled.

'Yes,' said Harry. 'Come on!' And he set off down the drive. His brother went reluctantly after him.

Walking turned out to be not such a bad idea after all. And, taking into consideration the size of his ears and the following wind, William arrived at school twenty minutes before his younger brother. There, in the playground, were all the old familiar faces (or rather, young familiar faces, as they were only the same age as William). He looked around for Angie, the brash and beautiful girl who had captured William's heart, as it said in those paperbacks his mother was always reading. But Angie was nowhere to be seen. Neither was Nick Knuckle, wild and attractive School Bully, who had been the bane of William's existence for the past however long it was. William looked around but could not find him either. But then, as he had no idea what a 'bane' was, he wasn't quite sure what he was looking for.

In another corner of the playground, out of sight of William, Nick Knuckle was holding 'Threatening and Scaring' practice with his two henchmen, Germ and Quiff. The school holidays had been long, and Nick was afraid that they might have forgotten every nasty thing that he'd taught them. (Let's face it, they'd forgotten everything the teachers had taught them.)

'Right. Let's try it again,' said Nick. 'And let's try not to forget the ugly face this time . . . OK?'

'Grr!' said Germ and Quiff in pathetic unison. (Together – badly.)

'Rubbish!' yelled Nick. Then, remembering there were two of them: 'Double Rubbish!!'

'Sorry, Nick,' one of the henchmen said quietly.

'Didn't you get any practice in the holidays? Didn't you scare anybody?'

'Yeah! 'Course we did!' they both lied.

'Oh, yeah?' said Nick, turning to Germ. 'And who did you scare?'

Germ thought, long and hard. 'Our cat,' he said. 'Nearly.'

'Nearly?'

'Yeah . . . like I was goin' to scare him . . . I had it all worked out and that . . .then, just as I was going to do it, like . . . he . . . er . . . ran off.'

Harry came through the school gate just in time to hear the bell for the start of school. Germ and Quiff were also very pleased to hear the bell, as it meant that they would be spared whatever punishment Nick Knuckle was about to dish out to them. Nick Knuckle was also pleased to hear the bell, as it meant that he didn't have to try to think up a suitable punishment for Germ and Quiff. Brash and beautiful Angie, the light of William's life, would have been totally amazed to hear the school bell, as she was at home, three miles away, in bed with flu. The list of people who didn't hear the bell is almost endless, as is the list of people who heard it but ignored it. Fortunately, the people for whom the bell was intended, the pupils of Palace Hill, heard the bell and responded to it, by filing into School Assembly.

After a hymn, to which no one seemed to know the right words, the Headmaster read the school notices. Among the usual day to day things such as the Caretaker's early retirement, the Art Teacher leaving under 'Suspicious Circumstances', and the Fifth Form Drama Club's umpteenth production of '*Charlie's Aunt*', came the announcement that the school was planning to form a football team. This was something that made many ears prick up. This was not something that William's ears did very easily, but even they had a jolly good try.

The formation of a football team was the talk of the school for the rest of the day. A notice was posted on the school noticeboard, asking for names . . . and after a very short time, extra paper was added to accommodate all the 'keen' footballers. Even the staff were surprised, until the Maths Master did the following sum:

Joining Football team = More Football Practice
More Football Practice = Less Lessons.

This resulted in the staff reducing the list, so that it only included pupils who could do the following:

A) Run.
B) Kick a ball.
C) Catch a ball.
D) Afford to buy their own kit.

But now the list consisted of only two names: William and Harry. Category (D) was dropped, and the list increased to twelve names, including Nick Knuckle, Germ and Quiff. Angie's Sensible but Boring Friend, Mandy, wanted to play, but no one would let her.

The 'team' then held a meeting to discuss the following:

1) *What shall we wear?*
Buying a complete set of football strip was out of the question. After a bit of discussion, some bright spark suggested that if they announced that the team would wear white strip, then they could all play in their underwear. A quick inspection proved that this was not a good idea. William offered to provide all the team with kit, as long as he was on the team. This was agreed by all.

2) *Where shall we play?*
As the school has no football pitch, playing 'at home' was going to be a problem. It said in the rules that all teams had to have their own pitch. After another bit of discussion, the same bright spark announced that his dad had a friend on the Council, and he could probably arrange to have some of the houses next to the school knocked down to make room for the pitch, but everyone thought that this would take too long. William offered to ask his father if he could let them have a field, as long as he was on the team.

'We don't want your old man on the team,' protested Nick Knuckle.

'No, no, School Bully. Not my father on the team.

Myself!' Once this was cleared up, William's offer was accepted.

3) *Ball*
This time there was no discussion. William made the same (generous) offer, and it was accepted straightaway.

4) *Positions*
After a bit of bullying, Nick Knuckle sorted out who was going to play where. Then someone realized that William had not been put in the team, which would mean no strip, no pitch and no ball.

'I know!' said Nick. 'We could make you Head Person in Charge of Holding the Coats. That's a very important position.'

'Yeah! It is! Yeah!' agreed Quiff and Germ, quickly responding to several sharp kicks in the shins.

'I must say, it does sound rather important,' agreed William, and he would have accepted, had not Harry pointed out that he wouldn't actually be playing football.

'Oh.'

''Ere!' said Germ. 'What about making 'im the goalie? I mean, nobody'd get the ball past those lugholes!' And so it was agreed, William should play in goal.

A quick phone-call to the Palace during mid-morning break established that William's father could let them have a field. In Cornwall.

'Where's Cornwall?' asked Germ, who had been away when they did Geography.

'Oh, it's in England,' William reassured them.

'That's a relief,' said Nick Knuckle, who was going off the idea. 'We'll ask Pranny where it is this afternoon.'

Victor (Pranny) Prannett B.A., was not looking forward to the afternoon's geography lesson. Teaching geography at Palace Hill was like trying to teach Kung Fu to stick-insects. He was buried in a pile of books when William's

MAP OF ENGLAND
CORNWALL
THIS WAY UP

hand went up, part-way through the lesson.

'Excuse me, sir, but where's Cornwall?'

Mr Prannett leapt up and glared at the class. 'Alright . . . which of you little thugs has nicked Cornwall? You're not going home till one of you owns up.'

'No, I'm sorry, sir, but I think you misheard me. No one has *taken* Cornwall. I was just wondering whereabouts it was in the country.'

'Ah! I see!' said Mr Prannett, frantically searching his desk for the correct textbook. 'Well, I hadn't actually planned to teach you about Cornwall today . . . er . . .'

After a bit of discussion which resulted in William promising to make Mr Prannett a Knight of the Order of Saint George when he became King, the teacher produced a map of Britain, and they all spent the next forty minutes looking for Cornwall.

Now, if you look at a map of Britain, you'll notice that it looks like someone with a big nose, sitting down. (The thing hanging out of the big nose is the Isle of Skye.) If you look along the person's leg, you'll find Cornwall. It's in the bottom left-hand corner of the map (or the top right-hand corner, if you've got the map upside down).

Having found Cornwall, and the first match being fixed for the following Saturday, the team made arrangements to travel to the pitch by train. William then suggested that perhaps they should stay after school and get in some extra practice, but the rest of the team thought that was a bad idea, in case they got too good.

The evening before the match, William was watching Nanny Goats ironing his football laces, when his father came in to ask if it would be alright if he came to Cornwall with the team.

'What as?' asked Harry, who was watching the maid embroidering his initials on to his football jersey.

'I could be a hooligan,' said their father, hopefully.

'You mean a supporter.'

'One of those. . . . yes.'

'We've already got some, thanks Father,' said William. 'Angie and Mandy are coming.'

'I thought Angie had flu?' chipped in Harry.

'She has. She's going to breathe all over the other team.'

'Well, I could be an Umpire,' continued their father.

'Referee.'

'That's the fellow. Yes, I could be a spare one of those.'

Harry and William grunted, which their father took to mean yes, so he went off to his study to swot up on the rules.

The following morning, William and Harry had hoped to sneak out without their father knowing, but William made the mistake of going and saying goodbye to him.

'Ready for the off, are we, Wills?'

'Well, yes . . . but. . . .'

'Good, good! I've been up all night studying the rules, and there's really nothing to it. It all seems to be a matter of adding the darts together and taking them away from 301, and shouting '180!' now and again.'

'But that's not football!' exclaimed William.

'Isn't it? Perhaps that's rugger. They're very similar.'

It took ten minutes for the Princes to convince their father that he'd stayed up all night learning the rules of League Darts. This almost made them late for their train. However, they finally boarded it with the rest of the team, and without their father. Thankfully they sank back into their seats.

The two Princes had never travelled on a train before, and William could not understand why the seats were covered in brown paper. Nick Knuckle then stuck his head round the door and asked what they were doing sitting on a couple of parcels in the Guard's Van. They joined the others in Second Class, and settled down to enjoy the ride.

After ten minutes, William was feeling peckish.

'Anyone fancy a bite?'

'Norrarf!!!' said the rest of the team, expecting William to produce one of his now-famous picnic hampers.

'Righto. I'll ring for a servant.' And before anyone could stop him, he'd pulled the communication cord. The train screeched to a standstill and several people fell over.

'What a terrible driver,' observed Harry.

'Alright! Which of you hooligans did that?' bellowed the guard as he lurched into the compartment. 'Was that you, Big-Ears?'

'Double beefburger and chips all round, please,' ordered William.

'I'll give you double beefburger and chips!'

'You don't have to give them to us. My detective here is quite happy to pay for them.'

Well, it took a while to explain things to William, but the end result was that the detective paid the guard to forget all about it.

'Right. And now I'll have a look at your tickets.'

A look came over William's face, as though the guard had suddenly started talking to him in a foreign language. This was the first he'd heard about tickets.

'What tickets?' asked Harry.

'No tickets, eh?' leered the guard, licking his lips.

'And no money either,' said the detective, who had been cleaned out.

'That's no problem, gents. No problem at all,' said the guard in a rather strange way. Two minutes later, William, Harry and their detective were standing beside the track, watching the train disappear into the distance. . . .

Are William and Harry going to get to Cornwall?

Are the Palace Hill team going to win the match?

Arsenal 2 Chelsea 4

Find out in the next exciting instalment of 'Palace Hill – The Book'.

LOAF'S LIBRARY

THE WIND FROM THE NORTH *by I. C. Blast*
THE REVENGE OF THE TIGER *by Claude Body*
EMBARRASSING MOMENT *by Lucy Lastic*
EATING OUTDOORS *by Barbie Queue*
LAYING CARPETS *by Walter Wall*
THE GREAT ESCAPE *by Willie Maykit*
SHIPWRECK *by Mandy Lifeboats*
SPARE THE ROD AND SPOIL THE CHILD *by Corporal Punishment*
LIVING IN THE ARCTIC *by S. Keemo*
SOLITUDE *by I. Malone*
BREAKFAST TIME *by Chris P. Bacon*

VISITING RELATIONS *by L. O. Granny*
CONTINENTAL BREAKFAST *by Roland Butter*
TRUE OR FALSE *by Adam Gessin*
HUNGRY CANNIBAL *by Henrietta Mann*
SHORT BREAK *by T. N. Biscuits*
HOUSE BUILDING *by C. Ment*
PONY RIDING *by Jim Carner*
END OF TERM *by C. Myra Port*
NO MERCY *by Ruth Less*
GRETNA GREEN *by Marion Secret*
SHORT OF FOOD *by M. T. Cupboard*
STAN LAUREL *by Olive Veradi*
COOKERY FOR BEGINNERS *by Egon Toast*
IRISH DOUBLEGLAZING *by Patty O'Doors*
SUNBATHING *by Tanya Tummy*
ACHING BONES *by Arthur Ritis*
APIARY *by Bea Keeper*
THROWING FRUIT *by Chuck Berry*
WELSH BISCUITS *by Dai Gestive*
SUN RISE *by Dawn Breaking*
ODD JOBS *by Ern A. Penny*
ALMOST LATE *by Justin Time*
GRASS CUTTER *by Lorna Mower*
PERSONAL COMPUTERS *by Mike Rose*
RECEIVE AN AWARD *by Oscar Winner*
FLYING BULLETS *by Rick O'Shay*
SAUCEPANS *by Stu Potts*
WEARING GLASSES *by Seymour Withem*
P.S. *by Adeline Extra*

TAPEWORM'S TEASERS

You can pick your friends –
You can pick your nose –

But you can't pick your friend's nose!
Know what I mean!

WHEN YOU WAKE UP IN THE MORNING— DO YOUR TEETH LOOK LIKE THIS?

THAT'S BETTER! NOW YOUR POOR MUM DOESN'T HAVE TO LOOK AT THEM!!!
'OO YOU LOOKIN' AT PAL?
YEAH! YEAH!
PRANG!
POOP!
KASPLODGE!
SPONG!
BLAD
BOOM!
SPLAT!

LOAF'S DAYDREAMS...
LORD GREYLOAF
CHAMP OF THE CHIMPS
IN
BUNGLE IN THE JUNGLE
I'M A REAL SWINGER
WOULDN'T IT BE RUBBERY

3

TARZAN

'What's on telly tonight, Mum?' Loaf shouted through the kitchen door.

'There's a film on – *Tarzan of the Jungle*,' his mum called back. 'You'll enjoy that.'

'Yes,' thought Loaf, 'I like Tarzan. I think he's great. If only I could be Tarzan . . .'

Jane flipped her duster with a sigh. 'If only these rubber plants didn't get so dusty,' she complained. 'And if only we didn't have a jungle-full of them. Trying to keep the leaves shiny is a full time job.'

A distant sound in the tree tops caught her attention. 'That must be Tarzan on his way home,' she said. 'He'll be dropping in any minute.'

She heard a loud cry of 'Ah-er-ah-er-aah! Ah-er-ah-er OW! Ouch! Aaah!'

Tarzan limped into view between the rubber plants. 'Me land on porcupine,' he said sheepishly. Jane sighed and bent down to pull the long spikes out of his foot.

Suddenly Tarzan pointed a finger at himself. 'Me Tarzan,' he announced, 'and you Jane.'

Jane pushed the pointing finger away. 'I know that, you idiot,' she said. 'We've been married for over a year. Now, what have you been up to all day?'

'Me swim across river,' said Tarzan. 'Me climb big mountain. Me swing through the trees . . . and me tear um leopard-skin.' He turned round to show Jane a big rip in his leopard-skin.

'Really Tarzan,' Jane scolded, 'that's the third time this week. Do you think leopard-skins grow in the jungle? You must stop all this swinging through the trees until you can do it without ruining your clothes!'

Tarzan hung his head while she shouted at him, but when she had finished he looked up. 'What's for um tea?' he asked.

'Bananas,' Jane replied.

'Oh no,' groaned Tarzan. 'Not bananas. I hate bananas. We had bananas Monday, Tuesday, Wednesday, Thursday, Friday . . .'

'We had fried bananas on Friday,' Jane reminded him.

'Fried bananas, fresh bananas, no difference,' said Tarzan. 'I fed up with bananas. They driving me bananas!'

'And you're driving me nuts,' shouted Jane.

'Nuts!' cried Tarzan. 'I go find nuts for tea,' and he rushed off into the jungle before Jane could hit him.

It was getting dark in the jungle, and it wasn't long before Tarzan was completely lost. He wandered around aimlessly for a while, but it was obvious that he'd never find his way home on his own. He decided to get help.

Cupping his hands around his mouth, Tarzan called, 'Ah-er-ah-er-aah!' as loudly as he could.

Soon he heard an answering call: 'Eek-eek-eek!' and something heavy dropped from a tree above him on to his shoulders.

'Argh!' shrieked Tarzan with surprise. Then he saw that it was his friend, Cheetah the Chimp.

'Cheetah,' he said, 'I lost. You must help me get home.'

Cheetah eeked cheerfully and led Tarzan out of the clearing. Two minutes later they were back in it again.

'Cheetah, this not way home,' said Tarzan. 'You take me wrong way.'

Cheetah eeked once more and led Tarzan back into the jungle. Two minutes later they arrived at the clearing again.

'Cheetah!' shouted Tarzan angrily. 'You go wrong way again. You try to make monkey out of me!'

Cheetah jumped up and down shouting 'Eek-eek-eek!'

Tarzan jumped up and down shouting 'Eek-eek-eek!' A large spider had just fallen down the back of his leopard-skin.

Just then the bushes parted and Jane appeared. 'What's going on, Tarzan?' she asked. Tarzan could barely keep still, but managed to splutter, 'Spider in pants!'

Jane quickly fished the spider out and then took Tarzan and Cheetah home. When they arrived they heard a dull 'thump-thump' echoing through the trees, the sound of drums.

'Oh no,' groaned Tarzan. 'The neighbours are having umnother party.'

A loud elephant call added to the noise.

'And they got *trumpeters* too,' he moaned, putting his hands over his ears. 'How will me be able to sleep?'

'Poor dear jungle man,' said Jane sympathetically. 'Can't you sleep? Do you have a headache?'

'Yes, I um certainly do,' cried Tarzan, clutching his head.

'Is it tense and blinding?' Jane asked.

'It certainly um is,' wailed Tarzan.

'Then close your eyes. I've got something to soothe it,' Jane told him.

Tarzan closed his eyes and Jane picked up a huge club and bashed him on the head. 'Oo-er,' said Tarzan with a stupid grin and he collapsed on the floor.

When Tarzan woke up a couple of hours later, there was no one around. The jungle drums had stopped and everything was still.

Tarzan sat up groggily. 'Wonder where Jane is?' he thought. 'Wonder where Cheetah is?'

A loud rustling in the undergrowth made him cheer up. 'Here they come,' he thought as he looked round. But instead of Jane and Cheetah, Tarzan saw a monstrously huge lion.

'Oh no!' he gasped in horror. 'A lion – and I'm just lying around for it to jump on!'

Tarzan leapt to his feet as the lion moved slowly into the clearing. He glanced quickly round for a way to escape, but he could see nothing . . . except a creeper hanging from a tree not too far from him.

'If I can grab that creeper,' thought Tarzan, 'I could swing across the clearing and escape through the treetops.'

As the lion tensed itself to spring, Tarzan leapt toward the vine. He grabbed hold of it and began to swing, but somehow he couldn't keep his grip and he started to slip, and then to fall . . . crash, right on top of the lion!

The lion growled with fury and tried to get out from under the person on its back but Tarzan clung on furiously . . .

'Loaf! Loaf! What are you doing? Get up from there at once!'

Loaf looked round to find his mother glaring at him from the living room door. He was lying on the floor, wrestling madly with the hearth rug.

'Oo-er,' said Loaf sheepishly, untangling himself from the rug. 'Sorry, Mum. I forgot myself, waiting for the film to start.'

'Waiting for it to start? It's been over for ten minutes!' exclaimed Loaf's exasperated mum.

'Oh dear,' said Loaf. 'I don't think I'm cut out to be Tarzan after all.'

TAPEWORM'S TEASERS

Did you know, it takes a centipede three weeks to wash his armpits, that's why he never bothers. Yuck!

TWEEMAN

THE SECRET DIARY OF TOILET DOOR AGED 1,333 and ¾

THURS 21 SEPT

Collected my fancy dress costume for She-la's birthday party. Saw her brother Tweeman, Disaster of the Universe, in the shop. He and the assistant had a fit of the giggles when I walked in, but I rose above them (I had my broomstick).

FRI 22 SEPT

Went to the Dogs' Home for lunch – but they wouldn't let me have a puppy.

In the afternoon bought She-la's birthday present. Wanted to give her a bottle of toilet water but Battle Cat wouldn't fill the bottle. Settled for a 'Do-it-yourself' Moccasin Kit. The instructions start, 'First catch your cow –' Everything else is provided.

SAT 23 SEPT

The big day. Decided to travel to the party in my own clothes and change there. (Had a bad experience once before when I went as a chimney and the bus conductor kept making embarrassing jokes about me sitting upstairs with the other smokers. Turned him into a Natterjack toad. He was furious. Some people just can't take a joke.)

Was greeted at Portcullis by She-la and gave her the present. She said she liked the gift paper (you can get

ON THE BUSES
BLIP!
ZAP!
EEK!
NIDDIP!

some really attractive bog rolls these days) and she went positively wild over the moccasin kit – apparently *junk* ethnic is in!?

Slightly miffed, I adjourned to the Gents to change. Boy-at-Arms was already in there – for someone with six arms he has terrible co-ordination. He'd drunk eight cans of Fizzi-Croaker, left it too late to go and was now desperate. It was appalling to watch; he had hands unbuttoning his jacket, hands polishing his glasses, hands undoing his shoe laces and in the middle there he was jumping up and down screaming, 'The flies you fools! The flies!' Next thing the hands were all slapping house flies out of existence like demented castanets, while he stood in the middle getting helplessly wet.

Changed in a cubicle. Difficult – as I had to paint my skull bright red with lipstick. The costume had real cream and custard in it. It was an inspiration to go as a sherry trifle.

SUN 24 SEPT

Put the Best Fancy Dress Trophy away in a drawer. Still feel sick when I remember She-la presenting it to me – for coming as a boil!? Even the pleasure of beating Tweeman into second place was marred when I discovered he wasn't supposed to be an ashtray – but me!

LOAF'S LAUGHS

Loaf was nearly knocked out when the Producer bashed him on the head with a full bottle of pop. Luckily for Loaf it was a soft drink.

Loaf's Mum: It's rude to reach for food at the table. Haven't you got a tongue in your head?
Loaf: Yes, but my arm's longer.

How do you keep Loaf busy?
Give him a piece of paper with PTO printed on both sides.

Teacher: If you found 10 pence in one pocket and 25 pence in the other pocket, what would you have?
Loaf: Someone else's trousers on.

Loaf: Will I be able to play the violin when my hand heals?
Doctor: Of course you will.
Loaf: That's good. I never could before.

Loaf's so stupid that when he shot an arrow into the air, he missed.

One day the Producer came into the studio carrying a small package.

'Been shopping?' asked Loaf.

'Yes,' replied the Producer. 'I've been to buy a bottle of toilet water for my wife's birthday tomorrow. Very expensive it was – this little bottle cost £15.'

'£15!' exclaimed Loaf. 'If you come home with me you can have all the toilet water you want for nothing.'

Loaf's Mum: What are you looking for?
Loaf: Oh . . . er . . . nothing.
Loaf's Mum: You'll find it in the tin where the biscuits were.

One morning the Your Mother Wouldn't Like It team were talking about astronauts.

'I'm going to be the first person to land on the sun,' Loaf announced.

'You can't do that,' said the Producer. 'You'd be burnt up.'

'Ah,' said Loaf, 'but I'm going to go at night.'

One day Loaf came into the studio with a penguin under his arm.

'Where did you get that?' asked the Producer.

'Found it,' Loaf replied.

'Well,' said the Producer, 'I think you should take it to the zoo.'

The next day Loaf came into the studio, still with the penguin under his arm.

'I thought you were going to take it to the zoo,' said the Producer.

'I did,' said Loaf, 'and I'm taking it to the pictures today.'

Producer: Where do you find kangaroos?
Loaf: It depends where you left them.

Loaf: Whenever I have a cup of tea I get a pain in my eye.
Doctor: Take the spoon out of the cup before you drink, next time.

Producer: Why are you always late for rehearsals, Loaf?
Loaf: Well, there's a sign at the corner of my street which says 'Go Slow.'

Loaf's mum told him to put on a clean pair of socks every day. After a week he couldn't get his shoes on.

One morning Loaf said to the Producer, 'It's funny. Yesterday our dog ate the kitchen clock.'
'What's funny about that?' asked the Producer.
'Well,' said Loaf, 'it's supposed to be a watchdog.'

Loaf went to the optician and asked if they sold monocles.
'Yes, we've just got a new consignment in,' he was told.
'Good,' said Loaf. 'Can I have one for each eye, please?'

SHARON, KAREN, DARREN...

...AND GARY

2

'STAR GAZING'

Sharon, Karen and Darren all come from different directions, and meet up with Gary, who is plugged into an even bigger personal stereo! Gary is still not in this world as Sharon, Karen and Darren all greet each other.

KAREN: Hello Sharon!

SHARON: Hello Karen!

KAREN: Hello Darren!

SHARON, KAREN AND DARREN: (*turn to Gary, together*) Hello Gary!!

From Gary: Nothing! The others look at Darren, and see that he is carrying a tennis ball. Darren starts throwing the ball to the others.

DARREN: Catch, Sharon!

Sharon catches the ball, and throws it to Karen.

SHARON: Catch, Karen!

Karen catches the ball, and throws it to Darren.

KAREN: Catch, Darren!

Darren catches the ball, and throws it to Gary.

DARREN: Catch, Gary!

Gary doesn't move a muscle. The ball flies past Gary, and from some far away place, we hear a scream! Darren shouts over:

DARREN: Oh, sorry, Vicar!

SHARON: That was fate, Darren.

DARREN: No, it was a tennis ball, Sharon.

SHARON: No, I mean, it was meant to happen, Darren! Do you believe in the stars, Karen?

KAREN: Do mean like George Michael and Michael J. Fox, Sharon?

SHARON: No, I mean like your birth sign, Karen!! It can tell you a lot!

DARREN: I was born under the sign of Taurus, Sharon.

SHARON: So was I, Darren!!

SHARON: What sign were you born under Karen?

KAREN: The Hospital, Sharon.

DARREN: You know, I've been told my future, Karen.

KAREN: What's that, Darren?

DARREN: I'm going to fail my exams, and end up pig ignorant, Karen.

SHARON: Did the stars tell you that, Darren?

DARREN: No, my teacher did, Sharon.

KAREN: Then I shouldn't take any notice, Darren.

SHARON: Do you know, some people can even read palms, Karen.

KAREN: Don't they have any books, Sharon?

SHARON: I never thought of that, Karen.

Sharon looks at Gary lovingly.

SHARON: Gary's palm said that he's going to be a brain surgeon, Darren!

DARREN: Is that right, Sharon?

SHARON: Yes! If he can pass his woodwork 'O' level, Darren.

KAREN: I hope he will, Sharon!

SHARON: (*big sigh*) And Gary and I are going to be married one day, Karen!

KAREN: Did the stars say that, Sharon?

SHARON: No, I did, Karen. You can't leave EVERYTHING to chance!

Sharon, Karen and Darren look at Gary, and each other. There's nothing to do.

DARREN: (*big sigh*) Let's go and get the tennis ball off the vicar.

TAPEWORM'S TEASERS

What's green and hangs from trees?

Giraffe bogeys.

LOAF'S DAYDREAMS...
ROBBING HOOD
AND HIS MERRY MORONS
"WE ROB THE RICH AND KEEP IT!"
ARROW ARROW ARROW! WOT'S GOIN' ON 'ERE THEN?
LOVE, THE SHERIFF OF NOTTING HILL
DEEP FRIER

4

ROBIN OF SHERWOOD JUNCTION

Loaf was gazing out of the window of the train when it pulled into the station at Sherwood Junction.

'Sherwood,' Loaf said to himself. 'That's where Robin Hood lived, isn't it – in Sherwood Forest. I wonder what it would be like to be Robin Hood . . .'

Robin Hood was walking through the greenwood with his band of Merry Men. Actually, they weren't very merry at all.

'I don't know why you 'ad to drag us all the way over 'ere,' grumbled Friar Tuck. 'I was quite 'appy at the camp, eating all that roast boar.'

'You're a real bore yourself,' snapped Will Scarlet. 'All you ever talk about is food. What *I* want to know is, when are we going to go out robbing the poor and giving to the rich?'

'You great wally,' Little John shouted. 'We rob from the *rich* and *give* to the poor. And as I'm the poorest person I know, I reckon you should all be giving to me.'

'You greedy lump!' exclaimed Friar Tuck.

'Who's calling who greedy?' cried Little John. 'You're the fattest, greediest person in the whole . . .'

'Come come, men,' said Robin. 'None of this arguing. We've got a job to do. We must rescue Maid Marion from the wicked Sheriff of Nottingham.'

'Why should we?' grumbled the Merry Men. 'We can't give *her* to the poor, so why don't we just leave her where she is?'

'Because,' declared Robin, 'she is to become my wife.'

'Oh well, in that case, if we have to,' the Merry Men grudgingly agreed.

Soon the merry band reached a spot overlooking the road along which the Sheriff and his prisoner would be coming.

'Right, men,' said Robin. 'This is the plan. We will ambush the carriage and shoot the guards with our bows and arrows. Then we can rescue Maid Marion and return safely to our camp in the forest.'

'Bows and arrows?' repeated the men. 'Bows and arrows? What bows and arrows? Have you got a bow and arrow?' they asked each other.

'Good grief,' said Robin in despair. 'Don't tell me *no one* brought a bow and arrows?' No one had.

'Maybe we could dig a big hole in the road and the carriage would drop into it?' suggested Friar Tuck.

'No time,' said Robin gloomily. 'We've only got a few minutes.'

'How about hoisting a big rock up above the road and then dropping it on the carriage – SPLAT!' offered Little John.

'Don't be stupid,' Robin answered crossly. 'Maid Marion would get splattered too, and I don't want a squashed wife.'

'I know,' Will Scarlet called out. 'We'll let Alan Adair sing to them!'

'Oh no!' yelled everyone at once. 'That would finish us as well as the Sheriff's guards.'

'There must be something we can do,' said Robin, racking his brain. 'But we've got to think fast – they'll be here any moment.'

The whole band of Merry Men sat down to ponder. What could they do? Suddenly Robin cried out.

'I've got it!' he shouted. 'A fool proof plan! A brilliant trap! It just needs you lot to act as bait.'

'You've got to be joking,' declared Friar Tuck. 'I've caught enough fish in my time, and I know that being the bait's the most dangerous part – it gets eaten.'

'You're so wet!' snapped Robin.

'No I'm not, but I would be if I were the bait!' Tuck replied.

'No one's going to get wet,' Robin told them. 'Now, are you going to do it or aren't you? Don't you want to save Maid Marion?'

Everyone started to say 'no', but Robin looked so fierce that they changed their minds.

'Right then, what you have to do is this . . .'

A short way off, the Sheriff of Nottingham's carriage was jolting along the forest track, surrounded by mounted guards. Inside, the wicked Sheriff was tormenting Maid Marion.

'At last I've got you, my dear,' he sniggered, 'and there is no escape. Soon I will make you marry me.'

'I wouldn't marry you if you were George Michael,' retorted the furious maiden, 'you great . . . gobstopper!'

'I'll stop your gob unless you're a bit nicer to me,' snapped the Sheriff.

'Ahoy, Cap'n,' shouted a voice from outside. 'Outlaws ahead.'

The Sheriff of Nottingham stuck his head out of the carriage. 'I'm not a captain, you gormless guard. I'm a Sheriff!' he yelled.

'Sorry, Cap'n,' answered the guard, 'but there is still outlaws ahead.'

'I should never have got guards from the Navy surplus stores,' grumbled the Sheriff as he climbed out of the coach to look.

Sure enough, there was a whole bunch of outlaws in the middle of the road, waving and blowing raspberries at the coach. When they saw the Sheriff though, they all turned and ran off into the trees.

'Ha ha,' sniggered the Sheriff, 'we've got them now. After 'em, guards! Don't let them get away!' As the guards rushed off he paused to speak to Maid Marion. 'We'll finish off those nasty outlaws this time,' he told her, 'and then you'll have to marry me!'

The Merry Men gathered around Robin in terror. 'They're coming, they're coming,' they cried. 'We've done our bit, can we go home now?'

'Don't be so pathetic and stay put,' said Robin firmly. Just then the Sheriff appeared through the trees, surrounded by his guards.

'At last I have you, Robin Hood,' he declared. 'There's no escape. Surrender or we'll cut you to pieces!'

'I'm going to count to three, Sheriff, and then I'm going to let you have it,' said Robin bravely. 'One . . .'

'Let us have what, you fool?' asked the Sheriff.

'Two . . .'

'I have two hundred armed men . . .'

'Three! Right, you asked for it!' Robin pulled out a photo which he waved at the Sheriff.

'What? Aaah! Flee! Flee! It's horrible, all is lost!' cried the Sheriff. He and his men turned and fled into the forest.

'Wow!' exclaimed the Merry Men. 'That was brilliant. What is it?'

'This?' said Robin casually. 'Oh, it's the ultimate.' He showed the photo to his men. 'A picture of Mike Reid!'

'Aaah!' cried the Merry Men and they too fled into the forest.

'Oh Robin,' said a voice from behind him and Robin turned to find Maid Marion. He rushed to hug her, but she was pushing him away, crying 'Get off! Get off . . .'

'Get off, you great lummox!' yelled the ticket inspector, trying desperately to free himself from Loaf's bear hug. 'What are you playing at?'

'Oo-er,' said Loaf, letting go very quickly. 'I'm sorry, you see . . .'

'Young people today,' growled the ticket inspector, 'I don't know what they think they are.' He turned and waved a finger at Loaf. 'Your mother wouldn't like it, you know,' he shouted.

'No,' agreed Loaf. 'No, she wouldn't.'

TAPEWORM'S TEASERS

What dog lives down the lavatory?

A Poodle! Get it?

PALACE HILL

THE BOOK

PART 2

THE STORY SO FAR:

William and Harry, Royal Princes and pupils of Palace Hill Comprehensive School, are on their way to play in a school football match, on a field (donated by their father) in Cornwall. They have been thrown off the train for not having tickets. Now read on. . . .

It takes a crisis to bring out the best in some people. Who was it – Socrates? Einstein? Me? – who said: 'When the going gets tough, the tough get going'? That's right, it was Billy Ocean. But, when he said it, he had not met William. Now, if he'd said: 'When the going gets tough, some people stand about looking pathetic', he'd have been nearer the mark, because that's exactly what William was doing now. Harry let him do it for ten minutes or so, then said:

'Come on, Wills old thing. We've got to get cracking!'

'But we don't even know which way Cornwall is.'

'Then you'll just have to ask someone the way,' replied Harry.

'Brilliant,' said William, very impressed. He thought for a moment.

'Harry?'

'Yes, William?'

'Which way's Cornwall?'

'I don't know!'

'But you said to ask someone.'

'I didn't mean me, you chump! I meant a local. Someone who knows the area.'

'Oh! I see! Very clever!'

'Come on, Wills. We'll just have to hike it to the nearest town. It's not that difficult. I've seen Uncle Edward do it on "*The Wide Awake Club*".

'OK. Let's get going.'

'Just a moment, sir,' said the detective, who had been standing quietly by. 'One small thing. There's nothing in my contract about hiking. I'm not trying to be a wet blanket, you understand . . . but . . .'

Half an hour later, when the detective had been dubbed the Duke of Rutland and given the prettier bits of the Isle of Wight, they set off in the general direction of nowhere-in-particular, in the hope that it would prove to be nearer to Cornwall than where they were at the moment. It wasn't, so they turned round and tried another direction.

Meanwhile, on the train, Nick Knuckle and the others were enjoying some of the many exciting things that can be enjoyed on a long train journey, such as sitting, looking-out-of-the-window, keeping-quiet-because-the-bloke-two-seats-away-wants-to-sleep. Oh! And thumping Germ everytime he said, 'This is exciting!' They had

Harry's and William's football gear with them, which they were guarding with their lives. At least they were, until some bloke who said he was a collector of Royal Memorabilia offered them a fiver for it.

'Well, they won't need them, will they?' reasoned Nick Knuckle, when Angie protested. 'I mean, there's no chance of them making the match, is there?'

Somebody once said something about 'Speaking Too Soon', but I don't think it was Billy Ocean this time. Anyway, whoever it was, Nick Knuckle had just proved him right. For when the train pulled into Truro Station (in Cornwall), Harry and William were there to meet it. Of course, it had not been easy to get to Cornwall by road, and they had had to use a certain amount of bribery to get people to help them. Harry kept a list and, in all, it had cost them: fourteen Knighthoods, six Life Peerages, three proposals of marriage, and a whole boxful of OBEs. They even had to promise to get one person a 'Jim'll Fix It' badge. Anyway, they made it to the station, where the rest of the team were:

A) Pleased to see them because it meant they had a full team.

B) Not pleased to see them, because Nick Knuckle had said that they wouldn't make the match and therefore it was OK to flog their gear.

Anyway, they were all together – that was the main thing. They made their way to the field.

'Field' is right. I mean, if you'd walked through the broken gate at 'Little Bottom Farm' (as the team did), and looked at the thing in front of you (as they did), you would have said, 'Oh look. A field,' (as they did). You wouldn't have said, 'Oh look. A football pitch, fully equipped with posts, stadium, refreshment tent, and Public Conveniences,' (and neither did they).

But you may remember that William had asked his father for a field. And that's what he had given them.

Deciding whose coats to use for the goalposts can be a tricky business. Unless, of course, you're Nick Knuckle and you have the gift of being able to persuade people, with only the minimum amount of force, to lend you their coats. Or unless you have Harry and William on your team. They offered their coats, saying that it was an honour and, since Sir Walter Raleigh had lent his cloak to Queen Elizabeth I, it was the least they could do. (I think it was just after that that she stuck him in the Tower, where he put his time to good use by inventing the bicycle.)

So, sorting the goalpost problem was not too tricky. Getting rid of the goats was.

'Look, chaps,' said Harry, as the team stood around wondering what to do. 'We've got a bit of time before the other team arrive. There's eleven of us . . .'

'Fourteen,' interrupted Angie, who couldn't count.

'Thirteen, actually,' said William, who could.

'Sorry. Yes, thirteen. There's thirteen of us, and only six goats. We should be able to round them up easily.'

Twenty minutes later, Harry was glad that he'd said 'should'. They decided to leave the goats where they were and play round them.

Then there was the question of the missing football gear. Nick Knuckle span a ludicrous story about the train being held up by a gang of International Football-Kit Thieves, and only getting free by handing over the Princes' football gear. William and Harry believed the story totally. They were trying to solve the problem when the other team arrived and solved it for them. Apparently they were two boys short, because Strikin Major and Strikin Minor had both gone down with mumps. So it was agreed that Harry would play for the other side and William, as goalkeeper, could wear his own clothes.

'You won't get anywhere near our goal, anyway,'

boasted Germ, which caused a fight to start. This was broken up by a couple of the goats. The teams then got changed behind trees and in bushes, which amused the two girls. It also distracted the goats, and by the end of the match they had eaten most of the clothes.

Once changed, the teams took to the field. Then they realized that neither side had brought a referee with them.

'Perhaps we should have brought Father after all,' said William.

'I could be ref as well as play,' suggested Nick Knuckle. But the other side weren't too keen on this idea. Just then, an old man with a dog passed by. A Life Peerage later he had agreed to be the ref, as long as he could do it from the touchline as he was a bit old for running about.

The other team, who were from the Cyril Smith Comprehensive School (and called 'Cyril Smith Athletic'), won the toss, and decided to play down-hill. 'Palace Hill United' (William had wanted to call the team 'Palace Hill Wednesday', but was out-voted) were very worried about their chances, until Nick Knuckle reassured them.

'Listen,' he said. 'With 'Arry on their side, they don't stand a chance. He can't play to save his life!' Which was true. He couldn't. However, Nick had not reckoned on the detective. You see, Royal Detectives are trained to protect The Royal Person at all times. This means preventing anyone getting within two yards of them. So, every time one of the 'Athletics' passed the ball to Harry (which was often), and one of the 'Uniteds' went to tackle him, the detective stepped in and 'sorted them out' (know what I mean?). None of this was seen by the ref, who had fallen asleep against a tree, although it did make his dog bark, which in turn caused the goats to run around chasing everybody.

A FIELD, CORNWALL
CIVILISATION
COME IN THE FLYING SQUAD!

In no time at all, the 'Athletics' were winning 15–0. All scored by Harry.

'Don't kick so hard, Harry,' complained William. 'After all, I'm the one who has to fetch the ball.'

'You're supposed to be tryin' to stop it!' moaned Nick Knuckle, who had just been 'sorted out' by the detective for the tenth time.

'Oh, come on, you chaps, it's only a game,' said Harry, making it 16–0. Who knows what the score would have been, if the ploughs hadn't arrived and ploughed up the field.

Things were pretty quiet on the walk back to London. (The goats had eaten the team's train tickets, which were in the team's trouser pockets.) No one was talking to Harry, except William, who reckoned that blood was thicker than football.

'It's not thicker than you,' moaned Quiff, who suspected that the detective had broken his arm.

No one was talking to the girls who, when they saw which way the game was going had started cheering for the other side.

'Well, if we hadn't, we'd have had nothing to do,' they reasoned.

It was a very, very, very long time before anyone at Palace Hill Comprehensive suggested forming a football team again. In fact, it was never mentioned again.

'How long is "never",' wondered William, as he put on his best suit. His parents were taking him to see a musical called '*Time*'. Perhaps he'd understand this 'time' business after he'd seen the musical, and be able to start wearing his watch. Perhaps he'd get a chance to meet Cliff Richard – he must know all about 'time'. After all, he'd been around for an awfully long bit of it.

NOW!
A GREAT NEW CURE FOR SPOTS
A CARDBOARD BOX!
BEFORE
AFTER
GET ONE NOW!
● Top quality
● Everything you need
● Easily assembled
ONE SIZE • UNISEX
AVAILABLE IN SENSATIONAL LIGHT BROWN ! EYE-HOLES EXTRA !

TAPEWORM'S TEASERS

I went to a fancy dress party –
I put a cow pat on my head
and went as Supergran!

LOAF'S LAUGHS

'You stupid boy!' said Loaf's mum angrily. 'Didn't I tell you to watch that pan and notice when it boiled over?'

'But I did,' cried Loaf. 'It was at half-past one.'

Loaf's mum bought him two goldfish as a present, but after a week she noticed that the water in the goldfish bowl was very murky.

'Why haven't you changed the water in the goldfish bowl?' she asked Loaf.

'What for?' said Loaf. 'They haven't drunk the first lot yet.'

‘I went fly-fishing yesterday,’ said Loaf one morning.

Did you catch anything?’ asked Mr Briefcase.

‘Oh yes,’ said Loaf. ‘I caught a 3 lb bluebottle.’

Loaf had just come back from his holidays and the Producer asked him if he had been water-skiing.

‘No,’ replied Loaf. ‘I couldn’t find a lake with a slope.’

‘Have you got holes in your socks?’ Loaf asked Mr Briefcase.

‘Certainly not,’ replied Mr Briefcase angrily.

‘Well,’ said Loaf, ‘how do you get your feet in?’

Loaf in a chemist’s shop: I want three bars of that white soap, please.
Chemist: Scented?
Loaf: No thanks, I’ll take it with me.

Loaf: The Producer doesn’t know how much words can hurt me.
Mr Briefcase: Why, what did he say?
Loaf: Nothing. He threw a dictionary at me.

The doctor gave Loaf some pills to improve his memory, but Loaf couldn’t remember where he put them.

Loaf is buying a bicycle on an instalment plan. So far he’s got two wheels and the handle-bars.

Loaf is so stupid that if you say ‘good morning’ to him, he’s stuck for an answer.

Producer: Loaf, why have you got a sausage behind your ear?
Loaf: Oh dear – I must have eaten my pencil for lunch.

Producer: Name nine animals from Africa.
Loaf: Eight elephants and a giraffe.

Loaf's Mum: Why are you hobbling around the place?
Loaf: Because my shoes hurt.
Loaf's Mum: That's because you've got them on the wrong feet.
Loaf: But they're the only feet I have!

TAPEWORM'S TEASERS

What's the funniest sight in the world?

A centipede cocking his leg.